MARY IN AFRICA

MARY IN AFRICA
MESSAGES FROM HEAVEN TO CHRISTIANA AGBO

Written and edited by
Gerald Curran

Based on the work of Engineer Michael Oteikwu

Order *Mary in Africa* on-line or from:
African Fatima
P.O. Box 4453
Washington, DC 20017 U.S.A.

E-BookTime, LLC
Montgomery, Alabama

Mary in Africa
Messages from Heaven to Christiana Agbo

Copyright © 2008 by Gerald Curran

Library of Congress Control Number: 2008912174

ISBN: 978-1-59824-983-5

Third Edition
Published April 2011
E-BookTime, LLC
6598 Pumpkin Road
Montgomery, AL 36108
www.e-booktime.com

This book is dedicated to all those who seek truth.

CONTENTS

Introduction 9

1992 13

1993 17

1994 21

1995 35

Excerpt from the Original Foreword 47

Index to Selected Accounts of
Favors Received 48

Selected Accounts of Favors Received 51

Prayer to Our Holy Mother 86

References 88

Ordering Information 89

Description of Cover Pictures 90

INTRODUCTION

Although the title of this book is: 'Mary in Africa,' we will be introduced to Mary in a roundabout way. We will look through the eyes of a girl who has a particular relationship with Mary. The name of that girl is Christiana Agbo.

Christiana Agbo was born in March, 1980, and christened a few days later at the mission chapel in her village. She was just twelve years of age and still in primary school when the events that were to push her into the public eye began to take place. At twelve years, Christiana was a sensible girl, tall for her age, but rather shy and stubborn compared to the other girls of her village. The Agbo family belong to the Idoma tribal group that inhabits the hilly country near the center of Nigeria, somewhat to the south of the Benue river. This tribal group is one of the many tribal groups that live side-by-side in that part the Africa.

The Agbo family owns farm land at the edge of Aokpe, a village in a rather remote part of the country. It is twenty-nine miles from Otukpo, the nearest large town. In the early 90's Christiana Agbo was attending the village primary school. During the day she would be in class, but would spend much of her free time with her sisters and cousins. The group would help her mother care for the vegetable garden, or bring herbs and vegetables home for cooking. It was at one of these times that Christiana saw a beautiful woman. In Christiana's words: "…I was sent by my mother to a nearby farm to collect some herbs for her and to my surprise I saw some flashes. Then I saw a very beautiful woman standing in the air and she was smiling at me. She stood looking at me, smiling, without saying a word. I became afraid and knelt down but then she disappeared." On another occasion a similar thing happened: "One morning at about eleven a.m. I went to the stream with my sister to wash palm kernels. I heard an unusual voice saying to me 'go home quickly, you have a visitor'. When I went home I went straight inside, but could not see anybody. Suddenly, a very beautiful woman appeared to me. She was in a beautiful dress, with her head covered and her hands across her chest. When I saw her I became afraid and asked her: who are you? I was going to leave the room when she called me back and said: 'Behold, I am the Holy Mother, come! Do not be afraid. I will come another time to introduce myself to you and tell you what I want from you'." This was one of the first times the very beautiful woman, the Holy Mother visited with Christiana.

The unearthly appearance mentioned above would be the first of many similar events over the next four years. The woman, who called herself the Holy Mother, would mostly speak to Christiana Agbo in her native language, while 'prayer partners' would record her conversations in English. The prayer partners were mostly groups of girls, usually four, of high school education or greater, who were chosen for her by the Holy Mother.

The countryside around the village of Aokpe is a patchwork of hills and streams, with small fields of grains and vegetables nestling among stands of towering trees. At the base of these trees is a thick undergrowth, an undergrowth which surrounds every open space. Aokpe itself is surrounded by enormous trees. In the village center there is a huge spreading Acanthus and, during flowering season, this seems to hover above the ground like an enormous orange colored umbrella. It was at a location, about one hundred yards from this spot, that the first of Christiana's notable experiences began. The chapters and paragraphs which follow and which begin with one headed '1992', contain selections of Christian's impressions of what happened. They are reproduced here exactly as they appeared in the book: 'The Messages of Our Lady of Aokpe...' by Michael Oteikwu. That book was compiled from the written records of events at the village of Aokpe. The numbers at the beginning of each paragraph, on the following pages, relate to the year and date on which an event took place.

1992

Number 921001
"On a certain morning, of a day in the month of October 1992, my sisters and I went to the farm to weed the portion that was assigned to us by my mother. While there, suddenly, there was a flash of light. I stood up and lifted my eyes from the ground. I saw the flashes of light again. I asked my sisters: 'did you see the flashes of light'? 'What light'? They asked. They were the sun's rays, they concluded. Those flashes of light that I saw were unusual and special to me."

Number 921002
"In the month of October 1992, my mother sent me to a nearby farm to collect leaves (herbs) for her. I was on the tree, when suddenly I saw flashes of light; then I saw a beautiful lady standing above the tree. She was shining so bright; I could not look at her. I was so frightened, I climbed down and knelt down. She smiled and disappeared."

Number 921003
"On a certain day in the month of October 1992, I was in my room when suddenly two angels appeared to me. They were singing a song. I became afraid. I called my mother to come and see the angels but she could not see them. One of the angels said to me, 'I am the angel of peace.' After saying these words the angels disappeared."

Number 921004
"In October 1992, at about 11 a.m., I went to the stream to wash palm kernels with my elder sister, when I heard a beautiful voice saying to me, 'go home quickly, you have a visitor.' At home, I did not see anyone. I started praying the Hail Mary and the Our Father. Suddenly a beautiful lady appeared to me. She was so bright; she wore a beautiful dress, flowing from [her] head down and her hands [were] across her chest. I was running away from her, when she called me back. I asked, 'Please, who are you?' 'Behold I am the Holy Mother. Come, do not be afraid. I will come again to introduce myself more to you and [tell you] what I want from you,' she answered."

Number 921105
"The beautiful lady appeared to me again. She asked me: 'Where is your Rosary?' I brought it out and we prayed together. She was only saying the Glory Be to the Father [prayer]. 'I am the Refuge of Sinners, I have come to bring souls back to God. I want you to help me pray for the world. Will you accept?' I answered: 'yes'. After this she left."

Number 921106
"The beautiful lady appeared again and said to me: 'Collect a bucket of water, say the Rosary and put it [the beads] into the water and leave it in the room 'till the following morning. I will come and bless it. Anyone who has faith and drinks the water would be healed'. Then she touched the Rosary and blessed it. I asked if I should go and collect the water from the spring, she said: 'No, but by 6 o'clock collect a bucket of rain water and do exactly what I have asked you to do.'"

Number 921107

"This time she appeared looking tearful. I asked why she was not looking happy. She said: 'More souls are going astray. You have to pray.'"

1993

Number 930703
"On the 21ˢᵗ. July, 1993, at about 11 a.m. I saw a flash of light and suddenly the Beautiful Virgin appeared. She told me to pray and fast earnestly for the world. 'I will come, but not very soon'. 'My Queen is so beautiful,' I said."

Number 930804
"On Wednesday 18th of August 1993, I saw a flash of light. Then I saw [a] Communion in the midst of cloud. I heard a voice telling me to kneel down immediately. The Communion became real blood on the floor and was flowing gently. It extended to my knees. I got up to see whether it had stained me but there was nothing on my knees. It came together and became [a] Communion again. An Angel appeared and put it in a little cup and covered it. He then opened the wall of the room, put it there and locked it. Then I heard a voice saying that, I should pray for the world; that the room is blessed. 'Anybody who

comes here and prays with faith will be saved. Here people should always observe silence too.'"

Number 930805
"On Wednesday 25th of August 1993, Janet and I saw the flash of light then she appeared. 'I will do many things in St. Patrick's here. Pray always,' she said.

Number 931006 [The following two accounts seem to overlap. Perhaps one of them was not revealed by Christiana until some later time. Ed.]
"On Friday the 1st of October, I came back from Church service. A few minutes later, I saw two angels. They backed me. [turned around? Ed.] Immediately I saw them I knelt down, but they asked me to stand. They genuflected and the place where the Blessed Sacrament was kept opened like a door, then they removed the Blessed Sacrament from it. 'We have been asked to remove the Blessed Sacrament'. When they were leaving I heard the sound of a ringing bell. Shortly after this Our Blessed Lady appeared. She was shining so bright. I called my mother and so both of us knelt down before her. My mother asked me to ask her name again. Before I

could speak she cut in quickly. 'I am the Holy Mother and I will introduce myself more another time. My little children learn from your mother. Do not fast today because there is one thing that I am happy about'. My mother told me to ask her to perform a miracle so that people may believe. "'Tell your mother that she is the one who told me [asked me?] before. I promised long ago that I will come to purify my children. The name they will call me here will be a powerful name. I will do many things in St. Patrick's Church.'"

Number 931007
Again, on Friday the 1st of October, the Holy Mother re-appeared to Christiana. "...at 11 a.m. I saw a round object, like a ball, on the floor with flowers round it and Our Lady came and stood on it. I called my mother, so both of us knelt down. My mother told me to ask for her name. Before I could speak Our Lady cut in quickly and said, 'Behold, I am the Holy Mother and I will introduce myself another time'. She then held out her hand and we shook hands. Our Lady said: 'I will appear to purify my children'. Then I said: 'I do not know your name'. She replied: 'The time of giving my name has not yet come. The name I will bring will be a powerful one. I

will do many things in St. Patrick's Church, Aokpe.'"

Number 931008
"On Monday October 4th 1993, I was praying, at about 12 noon, when I saw flash of light; then she appeared, she was standing in the middle of a huge cloud."

1994

Number 940101

"Our Blessed Lady appeared and said: 'Tell Father Samuel not to worry since God is with him and he should continue doing his work.'"

Number 940102

"Our Blessed Lady said: 'No one can suppress the Holy Spirit.'"

Number 940103

"Our Blessed Lady said: 'I am very happy today.... My priests represent Christ and so should act like him. I will appear again when Father Samuel comes.'"

Number 940104

While praying, the Holy Mother asked Christiana and her prayer mates [prayer companions] to go and pray for the sick in Aliade. They had no money. Shortly [afterwards] a woman rode up on a motor bike and gave them money that enabled them to travel to Aliade.

Number 940105
"In the morning I saw the beautiful lady with the Rosary. She was praying it. I did not hear anything but I saw her lips moving and a great light was shining at her back."

Number 940106
On Friday the 28th of January 1994 the Holy Mother spoke to Christiana. "My peace, love, and glory will be seen in you if you walk and stay close to me. Open your heart and love like Jesus my Son and my heart, which is full of love for you. Love God who fills you with love and goodness. My children, He cares for you so much. Love him who has made you to be worthy to receive eternal life. Love your brothers and your sisters, love the sick ones, the poor sinners, especially at this time [when] hatred is scattered all over. Keep away from sin for it will only destroy and make you miserable. I want you to entrust yourselves to me. Pray all the time. Come with me, little children, in faith, love and peace. I

love you little children, pray fervently and increase your mortification and be very sorry for sins. Keep yourselves from sin and any thing that leads to sin. I am the mother of peace."

Number 940207
"In the early morning of Saturday 5th of February 1994, I heard a voice calling me at a distant place where the Lady appeared to me the first time. I ran there and saw an angel standing. The angel said: 'Today is first Saturday of the month'. He then gave me Holy Communion. The angel left and I began to pray."

Number 940209
"On Monday the 21st of February 1994, Our Blessed Lady appeared as earlier promised. 'This season is very important, [it is] a time to receive many graces from the Mother of the Church. This is the period of Lent, a period of sober reflection; a special time to reflect on the suffering of Christ and the time to receive many blessings from my son Jesus. The love He has for you is unlimited. Live in peace with one another, love one another sincerely. I want you to stay close to me through the light of the Holy Spirit.

If you pray from your heart to Jesus, your prayers will be answered. Pray for the understanding of the Gospel of the Lord'. She asked me to say the litany of the Blessed Virgin always. '…Jesus is suffering. Offer all your pains to console my divine son. Pray always to console Him. I, your mother want you to draw close to me and I want you to look to heaven, where your tears will be dried forever. Love your neighbors, give to those who have none; offer prayers with faith; pray for your neighbor who hates you. Jesus has saved you from the hands of the evil one. Keep away from sin.'"

Number 940210
"The Blessed Lady appeared with the crucifix of her son. She said [that] any time temptation comes, we should pray the rosary and not be afraid because she is always with us. 'Any time you pray with concentration, I hear it. My children, many of you worship but you do not know what you are doing. Draw yourselves close and do not forget the word of Jesus: "Love your neighbors as yourself". If you want to worship God sincerely, you must ask the Holy Trinity to show you the way. You will learn how to give your neighbors who have nothing. In doing the

will of God you will receive grace always from the Blessed Trinity. I am the Holy Mother, if you pray earnestly I will present your prayers to Jesus. As you pray for yourself, pray for others too. Keep yourself holy in the sight of God. Do not sin again for it is your sin that made Christ suffer. Pray hard, especially in this period of Lent. What God did for you through His mercy is extremely good and so it is not good for you to be in the hands of Satan. I am your Mother.'"

Number 940311
"My children, love like the Immaculate Heart. If you show love then the Kingdom of God has become yours. God allows sinners to live long so that they can amend their ways and return to Him so that there will be great joy in Heaven. My children, pray so that more souls will return to God and there will continue to be joy. I go around to win souls for Christ and this is the will of God. Those of you who believe and do the will of God are like light shining on the mountain. Make yourself a peacemaker in the midst of people that do not know peace so that they will learn from you and live in peace. Come to Christ, carry your cross and follow Him. Pray for the world.'"

Number 940312
"On Friday the 5th of March 1994, I was praying when suddenly the Beautiful Virgin appeared. 'I want you to make this known to everybody, to all my little children. Put yourselves, my children, in God's hands and let Him use you through the power of the Holy Spirit. God wants to use you in a special way. My children, in working for God do not expect any reward from people. Your heavenly Father will reward abundantly.'"

Number 940313
"On Wednesday the 16th of March 1994, the beautiful Lady appeared. She was brighter than ever. 'I am happy; thank you for praying the Rosary so earnestly. Continue to pray the Rosary. My little children show love like my Immaculate Heart. Those who show great and true love will see the Heavenly Father.

God gives you chances so that you may return to Him because there is great joy when a sinner repents. Continue to pray so that more souls will change their evil ways; so that there will be joy. Pray always with faith because with prayer you can command and achieve everything. My children, you are light shining on the mountain-top. Be good; be peacemakers in the midst of people that do not know peace; be [a] good example to people, be strong because when you fall those behind you will [fall] too. Pray always for the world. Be patient and humble yourselves; help the old people - those that can no longer help themselves. Always do things with respect and regard for others. Take care of yourselves, pray always, pray for sinners.'"

Number 940415
"On Wednesday 6th April, 1994, Our Blessed Lady came as she earlier promised: 'If you want to follow your mother, remove from your heart earthly things and you will hear Jesus speaking to you. Pray and unite yourself to the Sacred Heart of Jesus. Open your mind to God and be attentive. My children, do not have bad intention against your neighbor, rather, do everything with love of God and when you love, heaven is for you. Jesus will bless you when you love. I have come because of my children whom the devil has captured. I am the refuge of sinners.'"

Number 940516
"Our Lady appeared on 24th May 1994, in the morning, and asked me to dig a well that will bring water and to do whatever she asked me to do. An angel will come to point where the well will be located."

Number 940617
On Saturday 4th June 1994 there was an apparition of the Holy Mother: "My children, you are always going against the commandments of God. Satan is deceiving you, giving you the pleasure and impure desires to go against the commandments of God. Many of my children are not on the right path. When the sun starts heating greatly nobody can reduce it. You better make amend. How will they hear this message? Through the graces I will give to those who ask for it."

Number 940718
During an apparition to Christiana on the 1st of July 1994, the Holy Mother said: "Tell my children to come to me on the 4th of August, 1994 to receive graces from me. I will give graces to those who ask for it. I will come again

to give you a prayer. Whatever you ask with open heart will be granted to you." Christiana relates that: "I asked her to take mineral, the Beautiful Virgin asked me: 'what kind of minerals do you have?' We have Coke, Fanta, Malt etc. She smiled and thanked me: 'these are earthly things'. She waved at me for the first time."

Number 940819
The Holy Mother repeatedly foretold details about events that were to occur on the 4th of August, 1994:

1. She told Christiana on July 1st 1994: "Tell my children to come on August 4 to receive graces from me. I will give graces to those who ask for it."

2. She told Christiana to prepare for August 4th – her 'Day of Grace'.

3. She foretold to Christiana that she was going to receive Holy Communion from the hands of the angels of God on that day. She asked Christiana to inform the Bishop that he was to come, or send his priests, so that they could watch the events. Bishop

Usuh sent Fr. Emmanuel Ojaje Idoko with cameras and audio recorders and he stayed closely by Christiana for the whole time and recorded all the events of August 4th, 1994. He submitted his report to the Bishop.

4. A summary of Fr. Emmanuel Idoko's account is as follows:

"I went to Christiana's mother's room and started discussing with her secretary. Christiana came in. She was a very timid little girl frightened stiff of the crowd outside and didn't want to go out to meet them. She was often looking up. When I asked her what was the matter she said she was waiting for Our Lady.

Suddenly she knelt down and said 'Here Our Lady comes.' This was at 11.05 a.m. She was steadily looking up with her two hands in prayerful position in front of her. She was not talking any more. I was by her watching her; then looking into her mouth, which was open, there was a Host on her tongue and I photographed it. Then I asked her to bring out her tongue with the Host on it and she did, and I photographed it again. I called the commercial photographer brought by Fr. Samuel Ehatikpo from Aliade to come and photograph it and he did. When I asked her she said it was an Angel followed by the shadow of Our Lady that brought the Holy Communion and not Our Lady herself. We were still talking when she knelt down again, saying, 'Here Our Lady comes.' This was 12.15 p.m., and whatever I said to her, she seemed not to be sensitive to it, nor to my presence any more. Later she started speaking to me, explaining what Our Lady said to her."

5. Christiana described the main event as follows:

Christiana described how she received the Host from the angel: "I saw the angel bringing the Host and the Host was bigger than the one we normally receive. The more the Host came closer to me the smaller it became. When I received it, it was the normal size."

6. Christiana recalled what the Holy Mother said:

"She asked that those present sing: 'Ave Maria, Oh Maiden, Oh Mother' for her and they did." (According to Fr. Idoko the Holy Mother then gave a powerful message, which lasted for about an hour. He said the Holy Communion was at about 11:05 a.m. and the Holy Mother's visit started at about 11.15 to 11.25 and lasted up to 12.30 p.m.)

Christiana related this message: "These messages are for the people of the world who refuse to repent after several warnings. Most people are like pigs in dirt. Most people are covered with dirt in their eyes and they cannot see the dirt in their ears and they cannot hear. No amount of preaching will make them repent. Some cannot even understand what is being preached to them. I will give you this proverb. If a son of a very wealthy person gets leprosy they will take him everywhere and to all the hospitals to get him cured so that he could live with people again. If a child of a poor man gets leprosy they will go and build a house for him in the bush to live there. My children, don't do such things for it is not good. You should think over it seriously and try to understand the meaning of the proverb. My children pray that the Holy Spirit will enlighten you."

7. Jesus also spoke to Christiana. Jesus said: "The people of the world should stop talking about the sins of the priests to Him. He is sending this message to you because most people go about complaining about the sins of the priests; that they are not behaving well. I know my own and own know me."

Number 941020
On Friday the 21st of October 1994 Christiana related that the Holy Mother said: "Walk with me in the light of faith. What else do you want me to do, tell me; I have given all the love a mother can give. Walk with me so that I can show you the way. Pray for wisdom and the fear of God. Hold your rosary very tight and pray it faithfully. The evil one is at work and will work harder. Satan cannot defeat my children as long as they pray the rosary. Why do you worry yourself about the things of the flesh so much and not of God? Have the fear of God in your heart always. Without the spirit of God, you

cannot do His will. Walk with me and I will show you the way."

Number 941121
On Saturday 12th November 1994 there was an apparition of the Holy Mother to Christiana. Christiana says of that event: "I bowed to her, brought the rosaries to her for blessing, as she earlier promised to do. She blessed them all and I asked her to kiss my own for me, which she did. I said that the Parish Priest does not believe me and Our Lady said: 'Pray for him; he will come back to open a new day of peace. I love you, that is why I have come so that you can enter into my Immaculate Heart.'" Christiana asked the question: "Do you want us to sing and pray at the same time?" and the reply was: "Sing songs that will make you pray and meditate. My little children, Jesus came and died for you but you hardly think about His death. Listen to Jesus speak this to you: 'When they called me I gave them sweet wine but when I called them they gave me a bitter wine.'"

1995

Number 950101
In January 1995 the Holy Mother said to Christiana: "I have come to wish you Happy New Year. I have come to remind you of what Christ has told you. Love your neighbor and anyone you see around you. Offer reparation, pray for sinners, pray fervently to obtain graces from God."

Number 950302
On Wednesday the 1st of March 1995 the Holy Mother said: "You are very close to the season of Lent. The glory of God will always be now and forever. This is the time to make atonement and reparation. Let it come from the heart. Jesus will be pleased when he looks down on you. Pray always so that the kingdom of God will be in your heart. Keep yourself from all evil ways. Offer all your pains, all kinds of sorrows you undergo to Jesus. I will always receive graces from God for my children who ask for it."

Number 950303

The following is Christiana's account of what transpired on Friday the 3rd of March 1995: "We were reciting the rosary when suddenly our Blessed Lady appeared. 'Little children, I have come to warn you again, to repent of your sins. If you do not change your evil ways, God will be annoyed with you. There is going to be trouble in the world. God is going to chastise the world and it will be really terrible. The anger of God will really shake the foundation of the earth. It will be a great darkness. There will be great thunder and lighting. Nothing will give light but those who are faithful to Jesus will be given light. The evil one will catch many souls but my Immaculate Heart will triumph. In few years to come (1998) the devil will spread its error more than ever. There will be a lot of problems and confusion and many people will not know what is right again. The evil one will claim to be everything. Many will follow him to confuse the children of God. It will be a great darkness. The devil will come knocking, claiming to be your friend, but do not open. Call on Jesus always'. "I asked: what are we going to do? Our Lady replied: 'Pray and amend your ways'. I then asked: what are we to do during the great darkness? 'Be close to the Cross of Jesus and those who are faithful to Jesus will see light'. I asked Our Lady: when will it happen? 'The time is very short. Pray and stop sinning. Pray, pray always. The time is very short.'"

Number 950404
"You have to pray, pray and pray."

Number 950405
The following is the description, verified by Christiana, of events that occurred on Saturday the 8th of April, 1995, after the Holy Mother had appeared to her. Immediately Christiana saw the Holy Mother she greeted her thus: "Mediatrix of all Graces" [see prayer at end of book]. The Holy Mother said that Christiana should say three Hail Marys, which Christiana did. The Holy Mother then lifted up one of her hands and Jesus began to speak: "I have come to talk about Mary and the ways she obtains graces for you. Your trust in Mary should be immense knowing that by the decree of God her power is without limit. She is the special means of Grace by which you can approach God more faithfully. All that I could

give to Mary I have given her and all that she was capable of receiving she has received in fullness. If you ask for her help you will place yourselves in the very flood tide of divine grace. She is the spouse of the Holy Spirit and Channel of all Graces. You receive nothing which you do not owe to a positive intervention on her part. She obtains everything for you." While Jesus was speaking rays of light came from His heart and Christiana also saw seven shadowy crucifixes coming out of our Lady's Heart. Jesus then explained: "These seven crucifixes signify the seven painful sorrows she always shared with me." Jesus resumed His explanation: "The purpose of my coming is to explain her position in the church. She is the woman that whenever she whispers anything to God, He responds immediately. She is the woman with whom God shares His mysteries and she in turn communicates them to her children. When you pray you should give her all the honor that you can, for she brings before God all your requests." The Holy Mother then said: "Christiana! This is the one to whom I submit all your requests." Christiana then asked the Holy Mother the type of food that they eat. She received the answer: "This is an earthly question and not of heaven." Christiana then asked the Holy Mother if they take minerals. The Holy Mother then asked Christiana what kind of mineral do you have on earth? Christiana replied, "We have Fanta, Coke, Seven Up, Maltina, etc." They smiled at each other. When Christiana was about to ask the Holy Mother another question, she motioned to her to stop. At Christiana's request, the Holy Mother kissed her fifteen decade Rosary for her.

Number 950506
When the Holy Mother appeared to Christiana on Sunday the 14th of May, 1995, she said: "My peace comes from heaven. My little children, I want you to visit the Blessed Sacrament. While you are there listen and you will hear Jesus talking to you. Many people, even some of priests no longer believe in the real presence of Jesus in the Blessed Sacrament. Attend Holy Masses. At Mass, during Consecration, you see Jesus at the altar and if you ask Him with sincere heart you will receive many gifts, blessings and graces from him." Christiana said: "A woman asking for a child for years is worried and almost losing hope." Our Holy Mother replied: "Worrying is useless. Have faith in God, pray fervently and open up your heart to God. Do not pray [only] with your lips and the good Lord will

grant your heart request." Christiana asked about some departed souls. Our Holy Mother said we should pray for them: "Believe and practice what the Holy Church teaches; renew the vows of your baptism; remember to pray for souls in purgatory. Those who pray for souls in purgatory will be rewarded. When you go to hell fire, you are there for eternity with the devil and his agents. Only those who go to purgatory have the hope of going to heaven. Pray for them and you will be rewarded."

Number 950607
On Saturday the 24th of June 1995 the Holy Mother appeared as she had earlier promised. According to Christiana she said: "I love you little children. It is because of the love I have for you that made me come down to call you back from evil ways. Pray for peace in your family and the whole world. Pray for the Church of Christ. The devil is finding different ways to destroy it, but God is with his church."

Number 950708
On July the 16th 1995, the Holy Mother appeared to Christiana who said: "We were

praying the rosary when she appeared. 'My little children, I want you to live in love, faith and peace. Have faith in the word of God. Pray, pray hard, pray for the chosen ones of God, the Bishops, Holy Father, Priests and all children of God. Have love for Jesus, who was nailed to the cross for your sake and who still speaks loving words to you. Love your neighbors. The evil one is up to deceive you. Do not stop praying the rosary. It is the same love of Jesus that I have for you and that love made me come down from heaven. Pray, I want you my little children to console Jesus all the time and when you visit the Blessed Sacrament.'"

Number 950809
On Wednesday 16th August 1995: "We were reciting the rosary at the apparition ground when the Blessed Lady appeared. [She said]: 'Saying the rosary, you will know much about the life, suffering, the glorious resurrection and the salvation Christ brought to the world. The graces obtained while saying the rosary will enable you carry your cross firmly. The devil will fight you, to make you drop your cross. You do not have to be afraid or be overtaken by the fear of death; be firm. If you want to follow Jesus, my divine Son,

you will take up your cross, share in his suffering, and then share in his glory.'"

Number 950810
On Wednesday the 30th of August, 1995, the Holy Mother said: "Always do your best, my little children, to console Jesus. Pray for those who do not know and those who know but do not care. Consecrate yourself totally to my Immaculate Heart and I will hide you in my love and peace. I have come to draw souls back to God. My little child, make sacrifice and do lots of penance for souls who are on the verge of getting lost."

Number 950911
On Friday the 8th September 1995, the Holy Mother appeared to Christiana as she had previously promised. "My little children, do not ignore the Gospel. Listen carefully to the Gospel and meditate on it. My little children, pray for those who cause you pain, pray for those who insult you because you are doing the right thing before God. My divine son will reward you. You will suffer for the sake of others. Pray the rosary

always, the evil one is always moving about."
Christiana said: "She then gave us her blessings."

Number 950912
When the Holy Mother appeared on Thursday
the 21st of September 1995 Christiana was heard
to exclaim: "Oh you have come down to us
again." The Holy Mother then spoke to her
saying: "Call on Archangel Michael whenever
you are in trouble. Always remember to keep the
commandments of God. My little children, my
Immaculate Heart is your refuge. It is the refuge
of all the human race."

Number 951013
When the Holy Mother appeared to Christiana on
the 6th of October, 1995 she said: "Jesus my son
is in the Blessed Sacrament waiting for you day
and night. The person whose mercy is limitless,
go to Him with a sincere heart. He will pardon
you. He loves you so much; that is why He waits
for you day and night in the Blessed Sacrament. I
have come to call you back. Come back to your
God my little children and beg for pardon."

Number 951014
Christiana related that on Wednesday the 18th of October 1995: "I was on the third decade of the rosary when the beautiful Lady appeared [she said]: 'Listen to the words of Jesus. Go to Him and ask for forgiveness. Console Jesus. Love Him with all your heart, like he loves you.' The Blessed Lady then gave us her blessing."

Number 951115
Christiana tells us that on Thursday the 2nd of November 1995 the Holy Mother appeared and said: "Pray, pray, pray, pray the Rosary always. I am calling you my little child to come and listen to my messages and do what I ask of you. Pray because of the days that are coming, the great darkness."

Number 951116
Saturday the 4th of November 1995: On this day Christiana says she bowed to the Holy Mother saying: "Your peace comes from Heaven." To this the Holy Mother replied: "My little children, you always respond whenever I call you. My little children, pray because of the great period that is coming. Pray and consecrate yourself to

my Immaculate Heart. Pray, especially for the days that are coming, the terrible days, that I may cover you with my mantle. Pray for those the devil has captured, for those who no longer have the sense of sin. Pray that you may understand my messages. My little children, I want you to be consecrated to my Immaculate Heart. The devil is very prepared, but my Immaculate Heart will triumph and the devil will be defeated. God has given to me the graces, I want you to ask for these graces. Pray earnestly; especially the Rosary. I am happy as you always respond to my call. My children, I give you my blessings which will remain with you."

Number 951217
On Friday the 8th of December 1995 Christiana stated that: "Our Blessed Lady appeared when we were reciting the rosary [and said]: 'My little children, I have come because of you today. It is because of your love which I have in my heart that has motivated me to come down to you. Pray that I may hide you in my Immaculate Heart. My little children, you who respond to my call, please accept my request, pray the Rosary all the time. I want a church built in honor of me here'." Christiana then said: "Could you make weather

cool for us?" To which the Holy Mother replied: "Why don't you offer it to Jesus as sacrifice? My little children, those of you that do not attend the Holy Mass, please make effort to attend. I am always glad whenever Mass is celebrated, for it gives glory to God. Attend Holy Masses. It will bring you closer to Jesus." Christiana said: "Your children brought their petitions and their problems are much," and the Holy Mother replied: "It is through their faith that I will heal them, though not all of them. Pray, pray, pray my children, because evil is spreading. Calm yourselves down and pray. Wherever I come, my peace will spread everywhere, be calm, do not make noise. My little children, be patient. I give you my peace."

EXCERPT FROM THE ORIGINAL FOREWORD

The following lines are an excerpt from the foreword, written by the Vicar General of the Diocese of Otukpo, for the book upon which this book is based: 'The Messages of Our Lady of Aokpe....'

'These compiled messages of Our Lady, to Christiana in Aokpe, are messages delivered by an innocent timid girl of a non-suspecting age and state, who had no previous religious experience. As a first Rector of Aokpe Pilgrimage Center and one who personally witnessed the public phenomena in Aokpe, I had no cause to, and indeed did not see in Christiana Agbo, anything of an ambitious girl who just wanted to be noticed. I rather saw her objectively as a messenger who was relating the messages she received...'

Very Revd. Fr. John Adeyi
Vicar General, Otukpo Diocese
First Rector, Aokpe Pilgrimage Center

INDEX TO SELECTED ACCOUNTS OF FAVORS RECEIVED

1. A brother returned home after 25 years.
2. A woman was blessed with a child after praying at Aokpe.
3. "The Blessed Mother wants us closer to her."
4. Woman had "lost all hope" – then she had a baby boy.
5. A husband is relieved of hepatitis.
6. "The Blessed Mother had a hand in my child's delivery."
7. "I ran from pillar to post, yet God still heard my prayers."
8. "I am sure Our Mother Mary had a hand in saving us…"
9. One down – three to go!
10. Peace comes to a family.
11. "All should thank Mother Mary for me."
12. A daughter sends her mother – to give thanks in place of herself.
13. A daughter is saved from a cult.

14. Prayer overcomes a hopeless medical condition which had prevented a woman from having children.
15. A petition to the Holy Mother got a husband for a daughter and a job for a son – all in the space of four months!
16. She got a job by the power of the Rosary.
17. He was promoted after recourse to the Holy Mother.
18. Problems in childbirth – solved.
19. She was blessed with the baby that she had asked for.
20. Shy no more!
21. This woman regained her sight.
22. A scheduled Caesarian Section operation became a normal delivery – at the Aokpe Pilgrimage Center.
23. 'Whatever you ask for in prayer with faith, you will receive.' (Matt. 21:22)
24. Prayer to "Mother Mary" brings a daughter home.
25. A Moslem woman who ran to the Holy Mother received her help.
26. A woman received guidance as to her mission in life.
27. A government official witnesses extra-ordinary events.

28. A woman in "bondage" is freed from an evil influence.

SELECTED ACCOUNTS OF FAVORS RECEIVED

The following are true stories, based on testimonies of pilgrims and visitors to Aokpe. The testimonies are collected by the staff of the 'Aokpe Message', the official newsletter of the Aokpe Center Council. The spiritual gifts of the Holy Mother to Christiana Agbo and all those associated with the village of Aokpe result in blessings to individuals and families, near and far, and range from physical healings to the fulfillment of deep spiritual needs.

1. A brother returned home after 25 years.

Mr. Dominic Onoja lives about four miles from Aokpe, and had been coming on pilgrimage since 1994. He had written a petition and given it to Christiana Agbo during one of these pilgrimages. The petition was in connection with his brother, who had left the country for the United States about 25 years before. He wrote: 'My mother always cries for his absence, so much so that whenever he sends money she would not accept the money, but would wish to see him.' In order that his mother's wish might be fulfilled, Dominic had continued coming to Aokpe to pray and to beg the Holy Mother to grant his request (that his brother would come home, at least for a while). He had made his petition to Christiana hoping that she would intercede on his behalf. In December 1997 his request was indeed granted and his brother had come home. Dominic brought his brother to Aokpe where they prayed together. He is ever so grateful to the Holy Mother and is convinced that the Blessed Virgin Mary really answers all our petitions. He gives glory to God for His blessings.

2. A woman was blessed with a child after praying at Aokpe.
One of the beneficiaries of the blessings of the Holy Mother is a Russian woman, Mrs. Marina Aigomoh. Marina had been married in the early eighties and had her first child in 1982. Until she began her pilgrimages to Aokpe in 1992 she had been unable to have any more children. Her heartfelt prayer was to have another child and after one of her prayer sessions in 1992, an old woman approached her and told her that she

would be blessed with a child. Marina became pregnant after fasting and confessing her sins and, without pain, gave birth to a baby boy whom she named Emmanuel. When Mrs. Marina Aigomoh gave her testimony in August in 1996 she was accompanied by her daughter Rosaline, 14 years of age, and Emmanuel, three and a half. She gave the advice that others should take her experience at Aokpe with all seriousness.

3. "The Blessed Mother wants us to be closer to her."
Bridget Odikayor is member of the catering staff at the Ministry of Health, and worships at St. Patrick West End parish in Asaba. She has been coming to Aokpe since March 1996 and has found that her constant pilgrimages to Aokpe have brought her closer to God. Bridget was an eyewitness to the miraculous healing of a paralytic during the miracle of the sun which occurred during one of her pilgrimages to Aokpe and she believes that she herself has had her own personal miracle in the way God has answered all her private petitions. Bridget Odikayor seems to have more understanding of what has been taking place at Aokpe than the average lay person. For example, she suggests that the

apparitions of the Holy Mother are not as important as the messages that they carry. According to her, anyone who has been an eyewitness to the events at Aokpe should count themselves extremely fortunate. She believes that the Holy Mother wants to bring all her children closer to herself and to God, so that they might attain salvation. Bridget cautions that, going by what Christiana told us about Hell and Purgatory, we should all take heed and listen closely to the messages. She advises all Christians not to attach too much importance to worldly matters but to be humble. Women especially should teach their children the proper tenets of Christianity. She has a theory that a recent low turn-out of pilgrims at Aokpe is as a result of a high cost of transportation as a result of a fuel shortage and thinks that this is temporary. She believes that the apparitions at Aokpe are more significant than is generally realized.

4. A woman had "lost all hope" – then she had a baby boy.

Mrs. Elizabeth Oko, is a 32-year-old housewife from Otukpo town near Aokpe. It was her dream to have more children after two successful births but her dream turned into somewhat of a nightmare, she had not had another child for about five years – an eternity for her. As the years went by and no child came she became despondent and "helpless". Mrs. Oko sought help from several orthodox medical practitioners, but it was to no avail. She then resorted to traditional medical services and visited several of them - but there was no help from any of them. She was at "the end of her tether" when a friend mentioned Aokpe. By now eight years had elapsed since the birth of her last child and, believing that this was her last hope, she travelled to Aokpe in January 1996. Mrs. Oko prayed "seriously" over her problems, and offered them to the Holy Mother. Barely a month after her visit to Aokpe, Mrs. Oko became pregnant and gave birth to a healthy baby boy. Mrs. Oko attributes the birth of her child to the kindness of the Blessed Virgin Mary – that she answered her prayers. Mrs. Oko returned to Aokpe, with her new baby, on the 19th of April, 1997, to give thanks to God and to testify to His wonderful work of mercy.

5. A husband is relieved of hepatitis.
Mrs. Juliana Nwaneri is from Enugu, an old coal mining town to the South of Aokpe. Mrs. Nwaneri is a regular pilgrim to Aokpe and in

1997 testified to the things that the Holy Mother had done for her since she began her pilgrimages. That was not the end of it though because barely a week after she had left Aokpe after the Day of Grace, August the 4th, 1997 her husband had taken ill with severe abdominal pain. Her husband had requested Soya milk for the pain but, after he had drunk it, the pain became more severe. Mrs. Juliana Nwaneri had to rush her husband to a clinic manned by his brother. Afterwards, Mrs. Nwaneri brought her husband home but the pain persisted, there was no relief. The pain grew worse by the day and Mr. Nwaneri was then unable to empty his bowel. After a week at home his stomach was becoming distended and hepatitis had begun to set in. Mr. Nwaneri was taken to a hospital where he spent another week - without improvement. After that, he was transferred to the University Teaching Hospital at Enugu. Now, because Mrs. Nwaneri feared that her husband would die she prayed for the intervention of the Blessed Mother, she also brought a quantity of Aokpe Blessed Spring water and compelled her husband to drink it during and after each meal. Not long after this, Mr. Nwaneri was advised to go to Park Lane Hospital, Enugu, where he would undergo surgery. When it turned out that the cost of the surgery was going to be 40,000.00 Naira, a whopping sum that she could hardly afford, Mrs. Juliana Nwaneri turned once more to the Holy Mother in prayer. She could not afford the amount needed for the surgery and recourse to the Holy Mother was her only remedy. Meanwhile Mr. Nwaneri kept drinking the Blessed Spring water. After about another week the distended stomach started to flatten and the doctor who then came to see him admitted that he was surprised at the amazing healing which had taken place. Mrs. Juliana Nwaneri had this to say: "Ave Maria...I have benefited more from the Blessed Virgin Mary than from anyone else!"

6. "The Blessed Mother had a hand in my child's delivery."

A mother of five, Mrs. Catherine Nwadioke, is from Saint Peter and Paul's Parish, in Abakpa Nike-Enugu. When she became pregnant for the fifth time, she prayed to God and the Holy Mother to see her through - despite the fact that they could hardly make ends meet. In a dream the Holy Mother had warned her not to tamper with the pregnancy, and she had awoken at three in the morning and had promised not to do anything that would offend the Holy Mother. She decided to go to Aokpe for prayers and had been able to continue to do this every month until the eight month of pregnancy, when it became impossible. In another dream, during that same month, she dreamt that she fought with a local woman about a towel. The next morning, when she awoke, Mrs. Nwadioke started bleeding and it turned out that the very woman she had fought with in the dream was the one who would carry her to hospital. As they were going to the hospital Mrs. Nwadioke drank some of the Holy Spring water that she had brought from Aokpe. Before they had even reached the hospital her bleeding had stopped. When they had actually reached the hospital, the staff were ready to admit her, but Mrs. Nwadioke declined to be admitted, she picked up her things and set off for her house. The doctor had been amazed, but she knew she no longer needed a doctor - at least not at that time.

When it became time for Mrs. Nwadioke to have her baby her labor pains lasted for three days. It seemed as though she would not have an easy delivery. But finally, after she had prayed to God and called on the Holy Mother and all the angels and saints, she was glad to have an easy delivery of her child. With a certain irony she had said: "The Blessed Mother had a hand in my child's delivery."

7. "I ran from pillar to post, yet God still heard my prayers."

Mrs. Ann Angela [not her real name] had been on pilgrimage to Aokpe a few times and had always intended to tell the staff of the Aokpe Message the wonderful work that God had done for her. Each time she decided to give her testimony, a feeling of shyness overcame her and she retreated into her cocoon. On one pilgrimage, she prayed to God to help her to overcome this shyness and God heard her prayers and she was able to give her testimony. Her testimony gives us the following account.

Mrs. Ann Angela got married in February 1993. However, after three years of marriage and without having had a child, she became restive and began to wonder if things were all right with her. Moved by extreme anxiety, she started to secretly visit oracles and traditional medical practitioners - although at that time she was the secretary of her local branch of the Christian Mother Society. On one such visit, an oraclist placed a calabash containing some unknown objects of his trade on her head and asked her to confess her wrongdoings and chant some incantations. After this he assured her that pregnancy would result. However, when there was no sign of pregnancy, she was directed to meet a soothsayer at a town about fifteen miles away. This man was supposed to be an expert in the business of restoring fertility to childless women. The soothsayer told Mrs. Angela that the spirit of her late mother was responsible for her condition and, in order to appease her, she should offer her a goat as a sacrifice. Mrs. Angela was astounded by this revelation and she knew it to be false - her mother was alive, hale and hearty! The foxy soothsayer had been caught in his own "trot". It now dawned on Mrs. Angela that she was playing into the Devil's hands - going "from pillar to post". In her bid to beget a child, she had even managed to convince her husband, who was the church leader in their local church, to consult the oracle, the soothsayer and the traditional medical practitioner, along with her. In the course of their search they had spent all their money. They seemed to have exhausted all hope of begetting a child.

When Mrs. Angela's friends at the Christian Mothers Society learned about what had been going on they advised her to go to Aokpe and put her problems in prayer before God and the Holy Mother. At first she was reluctant to go. She was of the opinion that the 'Blessed Virgin Mary' would never visit some unknown girl in the tiny village of Aokpe. However, after the Mass one Sunday, she asked a friend the date of the next pilgrimage. When told that it was only two days away Mrs. Angela asked to be taken along, her friend was delighted to oblige. When they had arrived as planned Mrs. Angela was able to tell Christiana's mother about all her harrowing experiences. Together they prayed about her problem.

After Mrs. Ann Angela had done the penance and collected Holy Spring water, she left for home. It was the end of her pilgrimage. In that same month, her cycle "skipped" and she informed her husband. Mr. Angela was so delighted that he promised to perform the next pilgrimage to Aokpe. The couple arrived together in April 1997 and by May pregnancy was confirmed. Mrs. Angela gave birth in February 1998, and soon after that brought her baby to Aokpe. Mrs. Ann Angela expressed her great gratitude to the Blessed Mother and to God for the gift of this child. She wanted everybody to join her in thanking God for his great mercy and kindness.

8. "I am sure Our Mother Mary had a hand in saving us..."

Mrs. Elizabeth Ake is from Kogi State. On this occasion she and some friends were on their way to attend a pilgrimage at Aokpe. They travelled by car and fearing that they would be late for Night Vigil activities, their driver "stepped on the gas." Soon the car was approaching Ankpa, a town through which they would pass on their journey. Suddenly, as they passed a gasoline station, they saw what seemed to be someone hurling a huge trailer truck tire in their direction. Though they had all been praying before they approached this spot, they didn't think they would avoid a severe collision. Everybody in the car just gasped for breath in horror. However, just as suddenly as it had appeared, the giant tire changed its course, leaving them space to pass freely by. On arriving at Aokpe Mrs. Elizabeth Ake summed up the experience by saying: "I am sure Mother Mary had a hand in saving us from what would have been a ghastly accident. Glory be to Jesus - Honor to Mary!"

9. One down – three to go!

The lady described in this account made four requests to the Holy Mother and her Son, Jesus Christ. Out of four requests, Mrs. Juliana Amuta claims that the Holy Mother has so far granted one, perhaps the greatest one. The following is an account of what happened.

Mrs. Amuta's problem started in 1994 when both of her eyes began to ooze a liquid, at the same time she was unable to see clearly. She spent her small fortune in the state capital city of Makurdi where she sought a healing remedy from an eye specialist whose reputation ranked above all others in the state. This was to no avail. She was at the point of total blindness when, at last, she made it to Aokpe. There, in spite of her poor sight, Mrs. Amuta was able to "see" the statues of the Holy Mother which are at various places around the pilgrimage site. She just knew, with the eyes of her heart, that the Holy Mother would have the most beautiful eyes – even in her statues. Whether out of desperation or sheer faith Mrs. Amuta challenged the Holy Mother to cause her eyes to be, not as beautiful as Mother's, but to make them good enough to see clearly. She made this challenge on the 16th of July and by the 9th of September she could see clearly. Through the intercession of the Holy Mother and the constant use of Holy Spring water God had made it possible for her to regain her sight. Mrs. Amuta considers herself a chosen beneficiary of the Holy Mother's miraculous healing works at Aokpe. She believes that she has benefited more from intercessions of the Blessed Virgin Mary and Her Son, Jesus Christ, than from anyone else she has ever known.

10. Peace comes to a family.

Mrs. Margaret Okpeke is from a town near the village of Aokpe. She received a wonderful grace for which she was able to thank Our Holy Mother at the Aokpe apparition site. Mrs. Okpeke had had some domestic problems with her husband since 1993. However, she turned to Our Holy Mother in prayer, to ask for a solution. Soon her prayers were answered and a reign of peace and harmony between herself and her husband came into being. The family now to enjoys "absolute happiness" - by the grace of God.

11. "All should thank Mother Mary for me."

The healing for which Mrs. Jenebu Peter is grateful for concerns a pain in the knee, from which she had suffered for fifteen years. She had given up hope of ever using the leg properly until she started coming to Aokpe to pray to the Holy Mother. The prayers of Mrs. Peter were answered and those who knew of the agony that she went through were surprised that she was once again well and fit and could use the leg for every purpose. Mrs. Jenebu asks everyone who hears of her healing to thank the Holy Mother on her behalf.

12. A daughter sends her mother - to give thanks in place of herself.

Mrs. Theresa Mary Anefu came to Aokpe on behalf of her daughter who lives with her husband in another state. Though married to a Moslem, Mrs. Anefu's daughter made a solemn promise to God that if she got married and was blessed with four children, she would glorify God and give thanks to Mother Mary in a special way. She made this promise in a letter of request that she wrote to the staff at Aokpe about six years earlier. Now all her requests had been granted and, according to her mother, she has been reminded in an inner locution to keep the promise she made to God and Mother Mary. Although never having been to Aokpe, Mrs. Anefu's daughter resolved to thank God for all his blessings. When she was unable to find out the exact date of the pilgrimage, she sent money to the editor of the Aokpe Message so that he might buy a ram to offer on her behalf - at the Harvest Thanksgiving Mass. She also sent her mother as an advocate to Aokpe, on her behalf. As it happened, Mrs. Enefu's journey to Aokpe had a double purpose, firstly to play the role of advocate for her daughter, endeavoring to fulfill her daughter's promise to give thanks and, secondly, to make her own thanksgiving.

13. A daughter is saved from a cult.
Mr. Daniel Ejembi is a Catholic who belongs to Holy Ghost Parish, Eke. Mr. Daniel Ejembi's daughter was in a secondary school in Otukpo and had a girlfriend who was both very beautiful and very kind to her. After a while it was discovered that this girl was in a cult and may have been "abnormal" in some way. The father advised his daughter to use Holy Spring water

and holy soil [from the floor of Christina's bedroom] to protect herself. The girlfriend resisted and fought back, but Ejembi's daughter was protected from every attack.

14. Prayer overcomes a hopeless medical condition which had prevented a woman from having a family.

Mrs. Elizabeth H. Attah of Nassarawa State had been married since 1993 and was seriously looking for the "fruit of the womb." She happened to hear Father Anthony of her local church, when he was speaking about Aokpe. He had advised anyone who felt drawn to Aokpe to go and see for themselves what was happening there. Elizabeth felt unusually touched when she had heard news of healings. The problem that she would bring to Aokpe was the fact that she had been told that both her tubes (confirmed by hydro-integration tests) were blocked. Elizabeth was likely to remain childless all her life unless there was a divine intervention of some kind. When she had set out for Aokpe she was looking for that 'divine intervention'.

On arrival at Aokpe Elizabeth began to shed tears uncontrollably. She happened to arrive shortly before a "miracle of the sun" at which time the people present were invited to pray for their needs. Elizabeth, who had arrived in Aokpe during her monthly period said the following prayer: "If it is really you, the Mother of God, that is coming down here, let this be my last menses." By November the 23rd, 1996, Elizabeth had given birth to a bouncing baby, after a painless pregnancy. This baby was four and a half years old, and had almost completed nursery education when, in August 2001, Elizabeth brought the baby and an appreciation gift to Our Lady at Aokpe. Elizabeth of Nassarawa State had become another happy beneficiary of the blessings of Our Lady of Aokpe, the Holy Mother.

15. A petition to the Holy Mother got a husband for a daughter and a job for a son - all in the space of four months!

Mrs. Caroline A. Moru, a mother of nine, became quite worried because her 27-year-old daughter, Joy, was yet to get married. The daughter would often ask her mummy: "when would I get married?" To help solve this problem Mrs. Moru came to Aokpe in January 2001 and petitioned Our Lady of Aokpe with promises of what she would do if her daughter got married. In a couple of months the daughter did indeed get married. On April the 28th, 2001, she was wed in the Church with her husband. That was not the end of the story. Mrs. Moru made another petition: that a job would be found for her 30-year-old graduate applicant son. By May, 2001, Our Lady of Aokpe had granted this second request. Mrs. Moru now tells us that Our Lady of Aokpe is very real and waiting to answer peoples' prayers.

16. She got a job through the power of the Rosary.

Mrs. Agnes Okafor, a mother of three, from Otukpo, had been praying the Holy Rosary for a job opportunity. After a morning Mass in April, 2001, a Mrs. Okoko called her and told her that she would take her to a director who was looking for someone to employ. Mrs. Okafor met the director, and after the interview, he asked her to report in 30 minutes to start work. The work was at another town and they had to set out right away. Before they could reach their destination however, something terrible happened. On the journey, their vehicle was involved in a head-on collision on a very narrow bridge. Mrs. Okafor was saying the Rosary at the time and she attributes the fact that everybody was kept safe, to this fact. The accident was resolved to everyone's satisfaction, and she was able to start her job as planned. Naturally, Mrs. Agnes Okafor will always be very excited about the Rosary and Our Holy Mother.

17. He was promoted after recourse to the Holy Mother.

Mrs. Otaru has a son who had worked for a very long time without promotion. Meanwhile, his younger brothers were being promoted at their places of work. Mrs. Otaru called her son and discussed the issue with him and she told him to keep calm. She then handed the problem over to the Holy Mother. A few days later, the management began to argue among themselves and they called him in and also told him keep calm - that his problems about promotion would soon be looked into. He told his mother about this development - that the management had taken it upon themselves to look into the matter. She just knew what the outcome would be! When the day came and Mrs. Otaru's son did get his promotion she said: "There is nothing Our Lady cannot do. Ave Maria."

18. Problems in childbirth - solved.

When Mrs. Mary Anyebe had been pregnant for about four months, she started bleeding until she seemed close to a miss-carriage. Her doctor suggested 'D and C' and went ahead and carried out the procedure. After the D and C, Mrs. Anyebe discovered that the baby was still alive inside of her, so she went to Aokpe and spoke to Mama Christy (Christiana's mother) about her problem. Mama Christy told her to do the "penance on the knees" and, when the penance was completed, she went to the grotto of the Holy Mother to pray. As Mrs. Anyebe was praying, she felt gentle breezes begin to blow on her and she felt cool all over. Later she requested that Christiana's mother pray for her. Mama Christy gave her holy water and the soil that the Holy Mother had stepped on, to rub on her belly. To her surprise, on the following day, the bleeding stopped and on the 31st of October, 2001, she gave birth to a baby boy. Mrs. Anyebe made a donation at Aokpe as an appreciation for prayer answered.

19. She was blessed with the baby that she had asked for.

For many years Mrs. Durin Cheoma Pauline was without the "fruit of the womb." It seemed that both her husband her parents-in-law could no longer accept this situation. She had visited many hospitals and doctors and the last doctor she had visited told her to go for an X-ray and an operation but Mrs. Pauline had been unwilling to seek a solution there. One day, at the office where she worked, a brother who is a friend of Our Lady, Mediatrix of all Graces, saw how terribly disturbed she was with her problem and advised her to visit Aokpe. He told her that her problem would be solved through the intercession of Our Lady. When the date for her to travel arrived she claimed that the Devil had tried to change her mind about going. However, since she only had just enough money for transport, and a little pocket money, she said to her self: "the devil is a liar" and went ahead with the journey. Once at Aokpe, Mrs. Pauline said that she made the promise that if Our Lady interceded for her and if Jesus answered her prayer, she would return and give thanks to Our Lady, to Jesus and to God for a prayer answered. She would also donate the sum of 3,000 Naira. The twenty Naira pocket money that she had on her that day was donated as follows: ten Naira towards a candle and ten Naira given during the Offertory. The following month Mrs. Pauline received a great blessing from God: she became pregnant. Nine months later she gave birth to a baby boy. Though it was a long time before Mrs. Pauline was able to make the journey back to Aokpe, eventually God made it possible and she returned to make good on her promise.

21. Rose Akpa – shy no more!

Rose Akpa is from St. Stephen's Parish, Otukpa. Although she is a good Christian, her shyness had never allowed her to do anything special for God. She asked the Holy Mother to give her the gift of speech so that she so that she could speak of God in public, and sing and praise God with her voice. Within a period of eighteen months her request was granted and now, not only is she able to speak the words of God in public, but she is able to sing and give praise to God out loud.

21. This woman regained her sight.

Alice Ogege had bad sight and had been praying at her church for it to be healed, When she came to Aokpe to pray she made the promise that if she recovered from her bad sight she would thank God at both Aokpe and Ogege, her home village. When she did, in fact, regain her sight she indeed returned to Aokpe to thank God and made the news of her healing known to the Aokpe Message staff. She also made the news of her healing known at Ogege.

22. A scheduled Caesarian Section operation became a normal delivery at the Aokpe Pilgrimage Center.

The following are events that happened to Mrs. Martha Ogwuche, wife of Clement Sunday Ogwuche of Otukpo. Mrs. Ogwuche had her first two children in 1997 and 2000. Both these children were delivered by Caesarian section. For her third pregnancy, the doctor, who had been taking care of her antenatal clinics had confirmed to herself and her husband that this delivery would also be by Caesarian section. The doctor had advised her to come to the clinic a few days earlier than the expected day of delivery so that she could be delivered by Caesarian operation and thus avoid any complication that might arise if she had to first enter labor. This time, however, Mrs. Ogwuche had made the resolution that God would deliver her of her baby normally and she rejected the doctor's advice. Instead she would cry out to God and pray for Him to deliver her of her baby. She decided to go on the special pilgrimage on 'Our Lady's Day of Grace' anniversary on August 4th, 2003, and she arrived on Friday August 2nd with other pilgrims from Otukpo.

When the group had arrived at Aokpe, Mrs. Ogwuche, did the 'penance on the knees'. She fetched and began to use the Holy Spring healing water and she prayed to Our Lady trusting that Our Lady would deliver her of the baby.

On Sunday, August 4th, Our Lady's Day of Grace celebration, she was at a nearby stream when labor pains started. She was rushed to the pilgrimage centre clinic where the principal nursing officer recommended that she be taken to the nearby hospital where there were adequate facilities for a Caesarian operation. Before this could be organized, a midwife, Mrs. Elizabeth Oko, a Lady of St. Mulumba from Makurdi city, safely delivered Martha Ogwuche of a healthy baby girl. The delivery took only a few minutes and there were no complications. It was remembered that Holy Mother had told Christiana about Aokpe Holy Spring water: "People that have

faith and come with their sickness I will cure."
Afterwards, Mrs. Ogwuche gave thanks and
praise to Our Lady Mediatrix of All Graces. Now
she knew that if one trusts Our Lady of Aokpe
they can receive all the graces, blessings and
answers from God that they need.

23. 'Whatever you ask for in prayer with faith, you will receive.' (Matt. 21:22).

The Holy Mother has established August 4th
every year to be her special "Day of Grace."
Since 1994, the Aokpe Pilgrimage Center and all
the pilgrims present have celebrated this day in a
special way. On the 4th of August, at about 12
noon, the Holy Mother comes to Aokpe to bless
her children - the pilgrims gathered in prayer. On
the August the 4th 2002, Day of Grace, she gave
several messages through the visionary Christiana
Agbo. One of the messages which were given
had also been given in the past. The message was
this: "Those who are going to work for me ought
to have no money problems. When they need
money they should take their rosary and pray for
it." It might look too simple a way to access
money or to have success, but compare this
promise to the promise of Jesus Christ in the
Gospel messages: "Whatever you ask for in

prayer, with faith, you will receive." (Matt. 21:22). Or this: "If you remain in me and my words remain in you, ask for whatever you want and it will be done for you." (Jn. 15:7).

After hearing of the success of others in receiving favors as a result of prayer and petition to the Holy Mother a devotee, who wants to remain anonymous and who we will call Alex, decided to do a 100-decade per day Rosary Novena. That is about six Rosaries a day - for nine days. Nearly every day of the nine days he prayed the Rosary before the Blessed Sacrament and each day attended Mass and received Holy Communion. He was praying for enough money to meet his basic needs and the needs of his family and of the Church. He was also praying that he would be able to carry on with his chosen work for Mary, his Marian apostolate, and the commitments and responsibilities involved in that work. For about a year Alex had been discussing with a friend how to finance a business that he wanted to develop. A week after completing the novena this friend phoned him and asked him to come the following day to collect money for the business. Two days later the friend gave Alex 300,000 Naira saying that he would like the business to take off as soon as possible. What makes all of this more amazing is the fact that the money was presented as a grant and not just as a loan. His friend wanted to enable Alex to get his business off to a successful start, right away.

This testimony is just another example of the way in which the Holy Mother does what she says she will do. It is yet another confirmation of how she is at work at Aokpe and around the world.

24. Prayer to "Mother Mary" brings a daughter home.

Victoria Ekpa was worried that her daughter Evelyn had matured but had not been able to find anyone that she wanted to marry. She could not find a man that she liked. All the suitable men liked Evelyn but she did not want to marry any of them. Victoria Ekpa began to pray to "our Mother Mary" to help find a husband for her daughter and decided to request that a Holy Mass be celebrated on a regular basis for the her intention. She scheduled a full eight months of Masses to this end and continued crying out to the Holy Mother for help. In the meantime her daughter had run away from home, and had travelled to the administrative capital of Nigeria, the city of Abuja. Later on, Victoria Ekpa heard that her daughter had found a husband in Abuja and this raised her hopes. She was overjoyed when, nine months after the beginning of the series of Masses, Evelyn brought her man home. The couple held a formal marriage ceremony, had their first baby and today visit Victoria regularly. Victoria Ekpa believes that God has done a wonderful thing for her and that she could never thank our Holy Mother enough.

25. A Moslem woman who ran to The Holy Mother received her help.

Abai Ibrahim is her name and she is of the Moslem religious tradition. Her family is completely Moslem and they are of the Igala tribal group. Abai Ibrahim had come to Aokpe because of the problems she was having at home. At the beginning of one planting season a child of hers had to have blood transfusions. This had happened four times but the child had eventually died. Abai Ibrahim had struggled to save her daughter but now she had lost the child. She had also seen her farm only barely survive. When another planting season had come, her older daughter's child started suffering a similar ailment to the daughter who had died. This child also had to start getting blood transfusions. Abai Ibrahim was completely at a loss as to what to do. Then, seemingly out of nowhere, someone she happened to meet told her about Aokpe and said that they would bring her there. When this particular man had brought her to the Aokpe Pilgrimage Center she had prayed to God to save her grandchild, asking that the child would not have to receive any more blood transfusions. She collected Holy Water from the Blessed Spring and committed the child to God's hands. Abai Ibrahim prayed that the child would not suffer from the ailment again and pledged 100 Naira as an offering. Today, that child is "hale and hearty" and walking, and has not received any more blood transfusions. Abai Ibrahim depends on farming more than usual, because she is a widow. As her farm had been doing so poorly she committed this also to God. The following year she had a "wonderful harvest" which enabled her to feed her family properly. When she was able, she came back to Aokpe to thank God publicly - in the presence of other pilgrims. Abai Ibrahim was asked by a member of the Aokpe Pilgrimage Center staff whether she believed in the Christian faith. They were interested to find out how a Moslem could be interested in a place of Christian pilgrimage. Her answer was that she believes that there is a God and that there is God's presence in Aokpe. She said that she has to remain a Moslem and cannot abandon that religion because it is what is practiced in her family. She said when she was brought to Aokpe she was afraid that her prayer may not be answered because she was a Moslem, but that the person who brought her said that God would not discriminate against her. Her final conclusion was: "I am grateful that God has answered my prayers."

26. A woman received guidance as to her mission in life.

Mrs. Shio Enwonwu had been coming to Aokpe for nearly a year when she received what she believes were graces for a special mission from the Holy Mother. She now mobilizes families into prayer groups and enlightens unbelievers so that they come to believe. For Mrs. Enwonwu, the miracles of the sun at Aokpe are great evidence for anyone who is inclined to believe that the Holy Mother has been visiting her children with messages to aid them. She was recorded in 1996 as saying: "Even when the apparitions cease, I will continue to come on pilgrimage to Aokpe to receive the enormous blessings the Blessed Virgin Mary pours out."

27. A government official witnesses extraordinary events.

Those who experience extraordinary events at Aokpe include the young and old, the rich and poor, those of power and influence and those without power or influence. Mr. Moses S. Ugye is one of those with power and influence who witnessed several extraordinary events at Aokpe. A pharmacist by profession, Mr. Ugye served with the Benue state government in many capacities and retired as Director General. Following reports by some friends of dramatic occurrences and miracles attributed to the Holy Mother which happened on the feast of Immaculate Conception in 1995, Mr. Ugye decided to go with some family members to Aokpe.

Mr. Ugye's group first went to pray in the area of Aokpe where some of the apparitions had taken place. When they had finished praying and were on their way to another part of the village, they saw a middle-aged man rolling around on the ground, yelling in a strange language, and praising God. They discovered that this man had regained his sight after many years of blindness. At about the same time, they noticed that the atmosphere had become cool, and strange changes were taking place in the sky where the sun was being blotted out. The whole area became dominated by the color yellow and every now and then this would change to violet or green. The trees themselves were covered by a golden yellow shade, which also rested on the other people in the area. They also saw a crucifix superimposed above the sun. Mr. Ugye had another Aokpe surprise in store - his daughter's feet were healed of some stubborn and painful corns.

28. A woman in "bondage" is freed from an evil influence.

Roseann [not her real name] travelled from Lagos to Aokpe in October 1996. She was brought there by her younger sister who thought she might gain some benefit from the graces which were heard to be flowing from that village. Roseann seemed to be suffering from a rather severe form of psychiatric illness. She would throw terrible tantrums and fall into uncontrollable fits of physical aggressiveness.

She would curse and swear and shout obscenities. As soon as Roseann arrived in Aokpe she began a violent fit, lashing out and cursing, much to the dismay of those present. Finally, she tore off all her clothes in front of the onlookers. When some semblance of control had been established and they had succeeded in covering the woman's body, the onlookers decided that it was best that she should be bound hand and foot. They wanted to be sure that no one would be injured. Although this controlled her body movements it did not control her mouth and Roseann still shouted and cried, saying that she was weeping for what she called the "sins of Nigeria." At this stage her sister gave up and decided to abandon Roseann to the mercies of the Holy Mother and to the villagers of Aokpe, and she left for Lagos.

Christiana Agbo's mother, Regina, had always been someone to whom people turned for help with a practical problem. Now she was quite happy to take Roseann, bound hand and foot as she was, into her home. Mrs. Agbo gave Roseann water from the Holy Spring to drink, and they all began to pray for this woman with the strange condition. Everything remained in this anxious state for about ten days, by which time there was the providential arrival at Aokpe of two bishops. These were Archbishop Ganaka of Jos and Bishop Aje of Sokoto, they had arrived for a private pilgrimage. When the bishops were brought to see Roseann they felt sorry for her. They said some prayers and anointed Roseann with Holy Oil and Holy Water, after which she fell asleep. When Roseann awoke she was astonished to see a large gathering of people around her. The Bishops asked the crowd of people if, "in their sincere hearts" they agreed that Roseann should be healed and the people said "yes". At this 'yes' the Bishops went into a long prayer session - Roseann went into a deep sleep and her bindings were taken off. For the first time since she had arrived in Aokpe there was no howling and cursing and Roseann slept soundly all night long. When her younger sister and her mother came to take her back to her home in Lagos there was joy on every face. She who had been lost had been found.

PRAYER TO OUR HOLY MOTHER

(This prayer was given to Christiana by Our Holy Mother in the Idoma language. It has not yet been presented in English in a form with proper grammar.)

Lady of purity of heart,
Lady of good heart,
Lady of honor that humbles herself,
Sweetness of Angels,
Your heavenly wisdom and your patience surpass all others.
The whole of your life is purity of heart that has no stain.
Lady, the Mediatrix of all Graces,
Help us to do without delay the will of Jesus.
Make us worthy to receive the gift that has been given to us,
So that we will be Holy.
Give us the Grace to go and greet Our Lord Jesus.
Help us to be pure so that we can see heaven.

Help us to always do the will of Jesus,
So that we can share in His Glory.
Father, fill us with the Grace of the Holy Spirit.
Amen.

REFERENCES

Michael Audu Oteikwu, 'The Messages of Our Lady of Aokpe, Mediatrix of all Graces' (Otukpo: Central Planning Committee, Aokpe Pilgrimage Centre), the accounts of Christiana Agbo's experiences from 1993 through 1995. Used with permission.

John Beirne, C.S.Sp., "Am I going to heaven or not?" (Enugu: Snaap Press Ltd., 2000), p. 10.

ORDERING INFORMATION

Order the book 'Mary in Africa' on-line or from: African Fatima, P.O. Box 4453, Washington, DC, 20017 U.S.A.

Order a free DVD titled 'AOKPE' from: African Fatima, P.O. Box 4453, Washington, DC, 20017 U.S.A.

Order the book "Am I going to heaven or not?" (account by a noted missionary priest) from: The Aokpe Office, 547 Kingston Road, Ewell, Surrey, KT19 0Dl, England, UK.

Order the DVD 'Our Lady Visits Nigeria' (a video made at Aokpe) from: The Aokpe Office, 547 Kingston Road, Ewell, Surrey, KT19 0Dl, England, UK.

Order the book 'The Messages of Our Lady of Aokpe, Mediatrix of all Graces and Testimonies' (the book on which this book is based) from: Aokpe Centre, P.O. Box 503, Makurdi, Benue State, Nigeria.

DESCRIPTION OF COVER PICTURES

Front Cover Picture: Photograph of a statue of 'Our Lady of Aokpe' which was modeled on an artist's painting of the Holy Mother as described by Christiana.

Back cover picture: On the 4th of August, 1994, Christiana Ago received Communion from an angel. (Photographed by Fr. Emmanuel Idoko)

CPSIA information can be obtained at www.ICGtesting.com
Printed in the USA
LVOW121148080513

332815LV00001B/2/P